Dedicated to librarians,
who create the perfect "nest"
for hatching new readers

All rights reserved. Published in the United States by Crown Books for Young Readers, an imprint of Random House Children's Books, a division of Penguin Random House LLC, New York.

Crown and the colophon are registered trademarks of Penguin Random House LLC.

Visit us on the Web! rhcbooks.com

Educators and librarians, for a variety of teaching tools, visit us at RHTeachersLibrarians.com

Library of Congress Cataloging-in-Publication Data is available upon request.
ISBN 978-0-593-17652-8 (hardcover) — ISBN 978-0-593-17656-6 (library binding)
ISBN 978-0-593-17655-9 (ebook)

The text of this book is set in 19-point Neutra Text Bold.

The illustrations in this book were created traditionally and using a computer.
MANUFACTURED IN CHINA
10 9 8 7 6 5 4 3 2 1
First Edition

RACHEL IGNOTOFSKY

WHAT'S INSIDE A BIRD'S NEST?

AND OTHER QUESTIONS ABOUT NATURE & LIFE CYCLES

CROWN BOOKS FOR
YOUNG READERS
NEW YORK

Chirp! Chirp! Chirp!

All around the world, baby birds want their breakfast!

BAYA WEAVER, ASIA

BALTIMORE ORIOLE, NORTH AMERICA

GOLDFINCH, EUROPE

TAILORBIRD, ASIA

YELLOW-CHEVRONED PARAKEET, SOUTH AMERICA

YELLOW-BILLED DUCK, AFRICA

Bird parents rush to find food for their babies!

They soar above the clouds,

zigzag
through trees,

dive into the sea,

swoop down from cliffs,

CLIFF SWALLOW

hunt in the moonlight,

GREAT HORNED OWL

and splash across ponds!

MUTE SWAN

Birds return home with a tasty meal for their young. For many, this home is wherever they build a nest.

Some nests are way up high.

PLATFORM NEST

WHAT'S THAT BIRD DOING?

WHITE STORK

Others are hidden inside old trees.

WHERE DID THEY ALL GO?

CAVITY NEST

PILEATED WOODPECKER

Some birds nest down low, or even underground . . .

WILLOW PTARMIGAN

WOW!

SCRAPE NEST

PUFFIN

BURROW NEST

All birds begin life as an egg.
Eggs can be colorful . . .

EMU

AMERICAN ROBIN

CETTI'S WARBLER

ELEGANT CRESTED TINAMOU

or have spots and speckles!

PEREGRINE FALCON

GOLDEN ORIOLE

AMERICAN GOLDEN-PLOVER

Some birds lay many eggs, and others lay only one.

GOLDLINE CHICKEN

LAYS OVER 320 EGGS A YEAR, FERTILIZED OR NOT.

ABOUT 12 EGGS IN A GROUP.

GREAT SPOTTED KIWI

LAYS ONLY 1 EGG A YEAR.

EGG IS ALMOST THE SIZE OF THEIR BODY.

But how does an egg become a bird?

Why are birds important?

What's inside a bird's nest?

Before there can be an egg, a bird needs to find a **mate**.

It all starts with a courtship.

EASTERN BLUEBIRDS

Sound is how birds communicate.

Springtime comes alive with a frenzy of birdcalls.

Songs are just one of the many ways a bird finds its mate!

Some birds do a dance.

There are birds that are famous for their colorful displays.

Many birds give gifts to impress a partner.

There is even a kind of bird that builds a work of art!

There are birds whose relationship lasts only seconds.

ALL HUMMINGBIRD SPECIES RAISE THEIR YOUNG SOLO.

BYE♥

BYE-BYE♥

And birds that pair for a lifetime.

TOGETHER FOREVER♥

SCARLET MACAW ♀

Most bird behavior falls somewhere in between. Pair bonds usually last for at least one mating season.

When birds mate, the male bird fertilizes the female's egg.

Pair bonded birds will raise their young together.

To prepare for new eggs, birds build a nest. It's hard work, but worth it!

A nest will cradle the eggs and keep them hidden from hungry predators.

Finding the perfect place for the fragile egg is important.

MY NEST IS HIDDEN INSIDE THIS TREE!

TREE CAVITY

DRY GRASS, STRAW, AND WEEDS

ENTRANCE HOLE

FINE GRASS

NEST

TWIGS

PINE NEEDLES

Birds are born knowing how to build their nest.
Instinct tells them what to do.

Some build nests that are gigantic!

GREAT BLUE HERON

4 TO 6 FEET WIDE

LINED WITH SEAWEED, MOSS, AND FEATHERS

BRANCHES

BALD EAGLES PASS DOWN THEIR NEST TO THE NEXT GENERATION.

½ TO 4 FEET WIDE

TWIGS AND STICKS

There are birds that create complicated weavings . . .

REAL HIDDEN ENTRANCE

?

SPIDER SILK

PENDULINE TIT

HAIR AND FUR

FAKE ENTRANCE KEEPS OUT OTHERS.

SOFT GRASS

BAYA WEAVER

STRIPS OF LEAVES AND GRASS

TINY ENTRANCE

COMMON TAILORBIRD

STRING

PLANT FIBER

4 TO 5½ INCHES TALL

LEAVES

WHITE-NEST SWIFTLET

BIRD SPIT

2 TO 3 INCHES WIDE

while others' nests are teeny tiny.

1 TO 2 INCHES WIDE

RUBY-THROATED HUMMINGBIRD

THISTLE

PINE SAP

SPIDER SILK

DANDELION DOWN

AMERICAN OYSTERCATCHER

PEBBLE

SCRAPE IN THE SAND

SHELL

FLAMINGO

And there are those who make a simple scrape or mound in the dirt.

MUD

Once the nest is completed,
the female bird lays her eggs.

Birds sit on their eggs
to keep them warm.
This is called incubation.

EGG

Eggs need constant warmth to grow.
The nest acts like a cozy sweater.

WHAT'S INSIDE AN EGG?

An egg starts out as a single cell.

A fertilized egg has an embryo. This is an unhatched bird in its earliest stages.

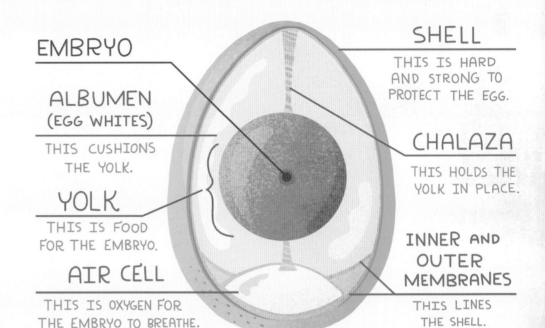

EMBRYO

ALBUMEN (EGG WHITES)

THIS CUSHIONS THE YOLK.

YOLK

THIS IS FOOD FOR THE EMBRYO.

AIR CELL

THIS IS OXYGEN FOR THE EMBRYO TO BREATHE.

SHELL

THIS IS HARD AND STRONG TO PROTECT THE EGG.

CHALAZA

THIS HOLDS THE YOLK IN PLACE.

INNER AND OUTER MEMBRANES

THIS LINES THE SHELL.

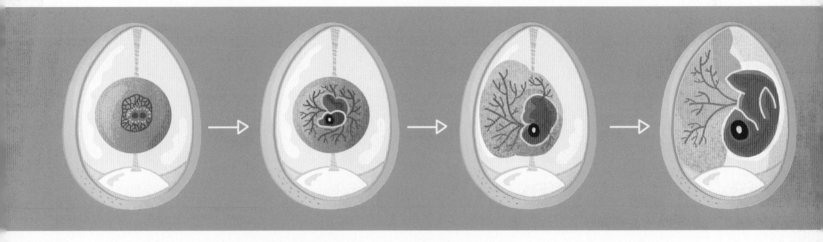

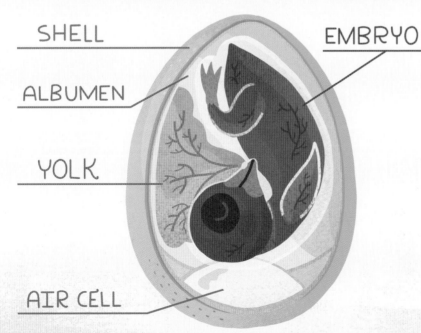

SHELL

ALBUMEN

EMBRYO

YOLK

AIR CELL

Cells divide and multiply, building different body parts.

Each part of the egg helps the embryo become a bird.

Birds must guard their nest.

Eggs make a tasty meal for many animals.

YUM!

COOPER'S HAWK

BACK OFF!

YUM!

STRAY CAT

Predators, like snakes, cats, foxes, and even other birds, see nests as a cookie jar, filled with goodies.

YUM!

GRAY RATSNAKE

Certain kinds of birds can be a big problem.

There are sneaky birds that lay their eggs in others' nests.

ADULT REED WARBLER

I'M YOUR BABY NOW!

BABY CUCKOO

THE REED WARBLER'S NEST

THE CUCKOO BIRD IMPOSTER HATCHES AND KICKS THE REED WARBLER'S EGGS OUT.

Birds squawk and fight to defend their nest.

ARCTIC FOX→

CAW!
CAW!

SNOWY
←OWL

Others lead predators away from the nest by faking an injury.

KILLDEER→

LOOK OVER HERE!

←EGGS STAY HIDDEN

SKUNK→

Some will nest next to a tough neighbor,

←VIOLACEOUS TROGON

←WASP NEST

while others find strength in numbers.

←SOCIABLE WEAVER

With time and care, a baby bird is ready to hatch!

① Soon there is a peck!

EGG TOOTH
TEMPORARY TOOTH FOR BREAKING THE SHELL.

② A wiggle!

③ POP

CHIRP

And a pop!

Many birds start life blind, bald, and noisy!

A newborn bird is called a hatchling.

Birds grow at different speeds.

Most birds that nest in trees are born completely dependent on their parents.

RED-TAILED HAWK

CARDINAL →

BIRDS THAT MATURE AFTER HATCHING ARE CALLED ALTRICIAL.

Many ground-nesting birds and waterbirds hatch with fluffy feathers and can walk.

BIRDS THAT HATCH MATURE ARE CALLED PRECOCIAL.

SNOWY PLOVER

TRUMPETER SWAN

Some birds even break out of their shells ready to swim and hunt for food!

Hatchlings grow their first fuzzy feathers and open their eyes.

They are now **nestlings.**

① HATCHLING

② NESTLING

③ FLEDGLING

Babies are fed constantly to become big and strong.

When a bird is nearly ready to leave the nest, it's called a fledgling.

ADULT

They learn to hunt as their colorful adult feathers grow in.

Old feathers fall out. This is called molting.

Once they are fully grown, birds soar through the sky, ready to take on the world!

MOLTING FEATHERS

FEATHERS

Birds are the only animal with feathers. A feather's special shape allows birds to fly!

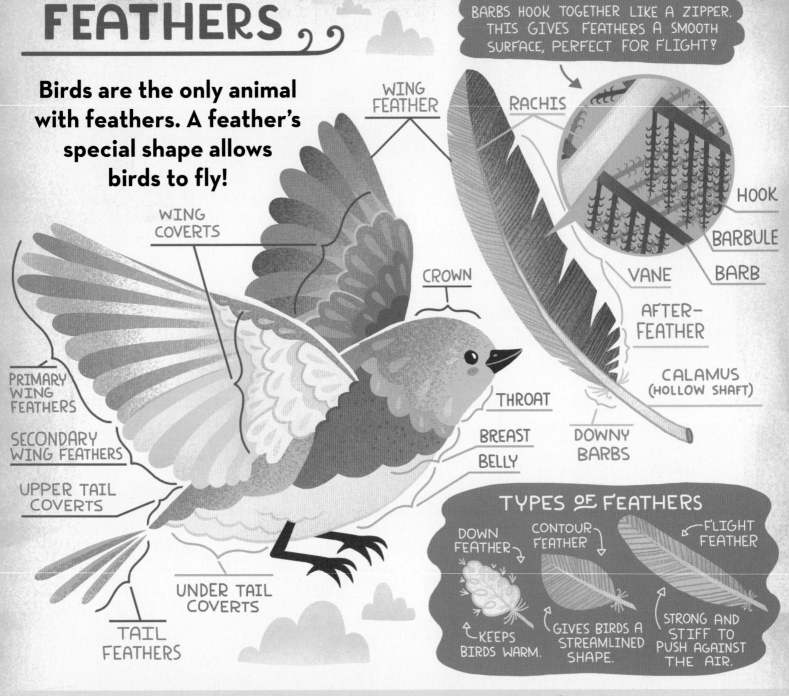

BARBS HOOK TOGETHER LIKE A ZIPPER. THIS GIVES FEATHERS A SMOOTH SURFACE, PERFECT FOR FLIGHT!

WING FEATHER

RACHIS

HOOK

BARBULE

BARB

VANE

AFTER-FEATHER

CALAMUS (HOLLOW SHAFT)

WING COVERTS

CROWN

PRIMARY WING FEATHERS

SECONDARY WING FEATHERS

UPPER TAIL COVERTS

THROAT

BREAST

BELLY

DOWNY BARBS

UNDER TAIL COVERTS

TAIL FEATHERS

TYPES OF FEATHERS

DOWN FEATHER

CONTOUR FEATHER

FLIGHT FEATHER

KEEPS BIRDS WARM.

GIVES BIRDS A STREAMLINED SHAPE.

STRONG AND STIFF TO PUSH AGAINST THE AIR.

Birds constantly preen to clean their feathers.

BIRDS PREEN TO KEEP FEATHERS FLAT AND INSECT FREE!

BIRDS HELP EACH OTHER PREEN HARD-TO-REACH SPOTS.

SCRATCH!

SOME BIRDS BATHE IN WATER.

OTHERS TAKE DUST BATHS!

GLAND

CERTAIN BIRDS HAVE A GLAND THAT MAKES A SPECIAL OIL FOR PREENING AND WATER-PROOFING FEATHERS.

BIRD ANATOMY

Birds are built for flight.

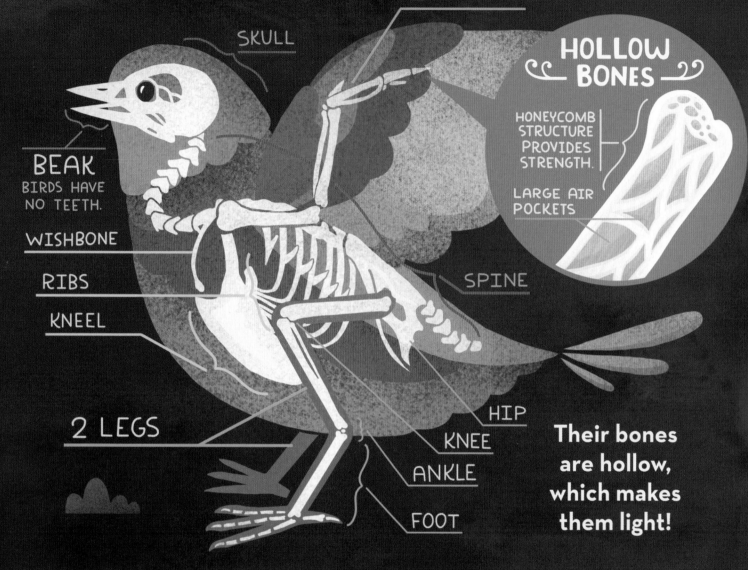

2 WINGS

SKULL

BEAK
BIRDS HAVE
NO TEETH.

WISHBONE

RIBS

KNEEL

2 LEGS

HOLLOW BONES

HONEYCOMB
STRUCTURE
PROVIDES
STRENGTH.

LARGE AIR
POCKETS

SPINE

HIP
KNEE
ANKLE
FOOT

Their bones are hollow, which makes them light!

Birds have different-shaped beaks, feet, and wings!

WOOD-DRILLING BEAK

MEAT-TEARING BEAK

WATER-FILTERING BEAK

SEED-CRACKING BEAK

PERCHING FEET

SWIMMING FEET

CLAWING FEET

RUNNING FEET

GLIDING WINGS

SOARING WINGS

ZIGZAGGING WINGS

HIGH-SPEED WINGS

KIWI

OSTRICH

PENGUIN

ALL BIRDS HAVE WINGS, BUT SOME BIRDS CANNOT FLY.

Birds need lots of food to power their flight.

There are birds that are fierce hunters. Birds of prey are carnivores that eat meat.

Birds hunt in the air, on the land, and in the sea!

Some are scavengers. They find dead things to eat and are part of nature's cleanup crew.

Most birds are opportunistic and will eat meat and plants.

Animals with this diet are called omnivores.

Seeds, fruit, and insects are a favorite meal!

Every bird is part of nature's complicated food web.

ANTS

ACORN WOODPECKER

ACORN

BEETLE

CALIFORNIA SCRUB JAY

BERRY

CATERPILLAR

SEED

CHIPPING SPARROW

NECTAR

ANNA'S HUMMINGBIRD

MOSQUITO

Birds are nature's gardeners!

Those that munch on plants will drop seeds as they snack.

Some birds hide seeds to eat later, just like a squirrel hides nuts!

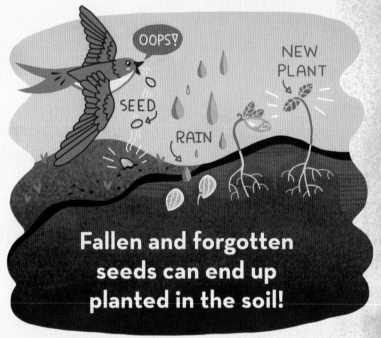

Fallen and forgotten seeds can end up planted in the soil!

Birds hunt insects that feast on crops.

They are nature's pest control.

Eating means pooping, and birds poop a lot!

Bird poop is a fertilizer filled with nutrients.

This creates rich soil for plants to grow.

Bird poop often has undigested seeds. With a "splat!" they get planted.

BIRD MIGRATION

The changing seasons trigger one of the Earth's biggest animal journeys, called a migration. Winter weather means fewer resources. Certain birds fly heroic distances in search of warmth and food.

MIGRATION EXAMPLES

① ARCTIC TERN

② SNOW GOOSE

③ RUBY-THROATED HUMMINGBIRD

④ SKYLARK

⑤ SIBERIAN CRANE

⑥ COMMON GREENSHANK

ABOUT 40% OF BIRDS MIGRATE!

How does a bird know where to go each year?

Birds navigate using the sun and the stars.

CANADA GOOSE

Birds also have special senses that can tell where the North and South Poles are, just like a compass!

Cold weather in fall tells migratory birds to fly south for warmth.

TIME TO FLY SOUTH!

SHIVER!

BRRR!

SHIVER!

TIME TO FLY BACK NORTH!

Seasons changing from winter to spring tell birds to return north.

Each year, many birds return to where they were born to build a nest and lay eggs.

① Adult birds court and find their mate.

NEST

② A nest is built for new eggs.

NESTLING

⑤

FLEDGLING

FLAP

FLAP

HOP

HOP

⑥

Babies grow feathers and practice flying.

EGG

HATCHLING

③ Eggs are laid and incubated.

④ Baby birds hatch and are cared for.

⑦ They take their first flight.

JUVENILE

ADULT

⑧ Fully matured, they are now ready to find a mate.

The cycle of life continues.

We have learned what's inside a bird's nest and why birds are important!

PEST CONTROL!

Birds help keep nature in balance.

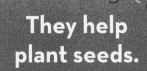

YUM!

They help plant seeds.

SPLAT

SPLAT

Bird poop returns nutrients to the land and sea.

Certain birds are keystone species. This means other wildlife depends on them.

KEYSTONE SPECIES: PILEATED WOODPECKER

OTHER ANIMALS LIVE IN THE HOLES I MAKE!

THANKS!

And there are birds that are pollinators.

HUMMINGBIRDS

POLLEN

They help plants make more seeds by spreading pollen as they eat from flowers.

Just like a precious egg, birds need our protection. There are many ways to help!

Turn your lawn into a diverse garden with local plants!

Be a responsible pet owner!

Clean up litter and stop pollution!

Protect our planet and wild spaces!

**Protecting our planet
starts with learning more!**

How will you keep exploring?

SOURCES AND RESOURCES

EDUCATIONAL ACTIVITIES

Go bird watching! You can even participate in bird counts that help scientists understand nature.

Learn more about birding here: audubon.org/birding

Ask an expert! Meet a scientist who studies birds (ornithologist) by visiting your local natural history museum, nature preserve, or national park. You can ask a museum guide or a park ranger about birds, too!

Build a bird feeder or a birdhouse. Natural resources for birds shrink every year, but we can help! Putting out feeders and houses helps birds find food and shelter.

For coloring pages and vocabulary worksheets, visit the author's website:

rachelignotofskydesign.com

BOOKS

Sartore, Joel, and Noah Stryker. *Birds of the Photo Ark*. Washington, DC: National Geographic, 2018.

Sibley, David Allen. *What It's Like to Be a Bird*. New York: Delacorte Press, 2023.

Taylor, Barbara. *The Bird Atlas*. New York: DK, 2021.